monographs on the ancient near east

volume 2, fascicle 4

the role of temples from the third dynasty of ur to the first dynasty of babylon

by

f. r. kraus

transation by b. foster

undena publications

malibu 1990

A Publication of
IIMAS
International Institute for Mesopotamian Area Studies

SOURCES AND MONOGRAPHS ON THE ANCIENT NEAR EAST

Editors: Giorgio Buccellati, Marilyn Kelly-Buccellati

These two series make available original documents in English translation (Sources) and important studies by modern scholars (Monographs) as a contribution to the study of the history, religion, literature, art, and archaeology of the Ancient Near East. Inexpensive and flexible in format, they are meant to serve the specialist by bringing within easy reach basic publications, often in updated versions, to provide imaginative educational outlets for undergraduate and graduate courses, and to reach interested segments of the educated lay audience.

MANE 2/4

The Role of Temples from the Third Dynasty of Ur to the First Dynasty of Babylon, by F. R. Kraus

Translation by Benjamin R. Foster

F. R. Kraus' "Die Rolle der Tempel von der dritten Dynastie von Ur bis zur ersten Dynastie von Babylon," an unpublished manuscript in German, was published in French in *The Journal of World History* in anticipation of inclusion in a scientific and cultural history of mankind to be issued by the International Commission for a Scientific and Cultural History of Mankind. The essay discusses in general terms the role of temples in early Mesopotamian society, then turns to more detailed consideration of the respective positions of temples in Babylonian society at the end of the third and during the first half of the second millennium B.C.

ISBN: 0-89003-240-8

Printed in the United States of America

UNDENA PUBLICATIONS, P.O. BOX 97, MALIBU, CALIFORNIA 90265

PREFACE

This translation of F. R. Kraus' "The Role of Temples from the Third Dynasty of Ur to the First Dynasty of Babylon" is made from the unpublished German manuscript from which the published French version was prepared. The English version adheres rather closely to the German in order to convey, as far as possible, a sense of the author's distinctive style. The text and notes have not been revised, except for the addition of three footnotes.

The article was first translated into English in 1974 for Undena Publications by Stephanie Serlin. Foster has retranslated the piece using Serlin's manuscript; final responsibility is his alone. The translator thanks Julie Rosenbaum, without whose interest he would never have become involved in this undertaking, and Cassis Henry, for editorial assistance.

The translator's particular thanks go to F. R. Kraus for his willingness to see his essay republished in English and for his reading of the translation.

Benjamin R. Foster

September 1990

TRANSLATOR'S INTRODUCTION

F. R. Kraus' 1953 essay[1] treats the role of temples in Babylonian society at the end of the third and beginning of the second millennium B.C. It discusses in general terms the role of temples in early Mesopotamian society, then turns to more detailed consideration of the respective positions of temples Babylonian society under the Third Dynasty of Ur and during the Old Babylonian period.

Perhaps because this essay was first published in a periodical in which appeared another essay by A. Falkenstein on the centrality of temples in early Sumerian society,[2] some readers[3] have referred to Kraus' work as if it defended the "Temple-State" hypothesis as first set forth by A. Deimel[4] and elaborated by Falkenstein in the context cited. Kraus, who did not know of Falkenstein's essay before receiving an offprint from the author on August 18, 1954, considers this an incorrect representation of his position.

Although almost forty years of scholarship have passed since preparation of this study, including substantial contributions by Kraus himself,[5] it remains a unique endeavor to compare and contrast the role of temples in the two periods concerned. Whatever their modification in details, the hypotheses presented here retain their timeliness and interest both for specialists within Assyriology and for historians concerning themselves with the problems involved.

B.R.F.

---

1. "Die Rolle der Tempel von der dritten Dynastie von Ur bis zur ersten Dynastie von Babylon," published as "Le rôle des temples depuis la troisième dynastie d'Ur jusqu'à la première dynastie de Babylone," *Cahiers d'Histoire Mondiale* 1 (1953/4), 518-545.

2. English version: "The Sumerian Temple City," translated by M. deJ. Ellis, MANE 1/1 (1974); original French publication in *Cahiers d'Histoire Mondiale* 1 (1953/4), 784-814.

3. E.g. I. J. Gelb, "On the Alleged Temple and State Economies in Ancient Mesopotamia," *Studi in Onore di Edoardo Volterra* 6 (Rome: 1967), 138f.: "unwittingly . . . contributed to a lopsided view of Mesopotamian economy. . . ."

4. For an assessment of Deimel's thesis, with bibliography of the relevant literature, see B. R. Foster, "A New Look at the Sumerian Temple State," *Journal of the Economic and Social History of the Orient* 24/3 (1981), 225-241.

5. For a bibliography of publications prior to 1980, see G. van Driel et al., eds., *Zikir Šumim: Assyriological Studies Presented to F. R. Kraus on His Seventieth Birthday* (Leiden: 1982), 485-491 (compiled by P. A. Siebesma).

THE ROLE OF TEMPLES FROM THE THIRD DYNASTY OF UR TO THE FIRST DYNASTY OF BABYLON[1]

F. R. Kraus

The Temple in Ancient Mesopotamia

The Bible and the Koran[2] have kept alive, until our own time, the memory of Babylon for a great part of mankind that, by and large, is unaware that it is the indirect heir as well to many of the intellectual achievements of the Babylonians.[3] For everyone who knows Babylon from the Bible it is inseparably associated with the "tower."[4] Yet, as Herodotus has already reported, on the basis of his own observation and inquiry, this tower was a temple.[5] The temple was so characteristic of the city that together they became legend, whereas almost every other recollection of Babylon faded from posterity.

As Europe, in fits and starts, began to rediscover that country, travelers saw the immense ruins of temples there as the most obvious remains of Babylonian cities, though what men like Benjamin of Tudela,[6] Schiltberger,[7] or Dr. Rauwolf[8] took to be the tower of Babel turned out later to be the similar temple towers of Dur-Kurigalzu and Borsippa.[9]

Modern excavations in Iraq, time and again, expose temples as the most significant, and often the only noteworthy structure of Mesopotamian settlements.[10] Thus tradition and research, literature and material remains prove unanimously that the temple held a preeminent position within the Babylonian city.

To probe the nature of this situation, the question has first to be raised as to what a Babylonian temple actually was. The most certain answer to this question is provided for us by the languages of the Sumerians and Akkadians, the two peoples of ancient Mesopotamia who inhabited Babylonia during the period with which we are concerned,[11] through the words they used for the concept "temple."

What we call a "temple" is, according to both Sumerian and Akkadian conceptualization, the "house of a god,"[12] and thereby belongs to the object category "house" like, for example, the house of a king[13] or a citizen[14] or other structures as well.[15] In most cases Akkadians and Sumerians render

1. Notes are kept to an absolute minimum and where possible refer to well-known handbooks. Articles and books are cited only by the numbers assigned to them in the appended bibliography, alphabetically arranged by author. Citations of original texts are in square brackets, other sources in parentheses.

2. *Sura* 2 verse 101.

3. (64), 156-158.

4. Genesis 11:4f.

5. I 181.

6. (103), 339 Nr. 65.

7. (103), 340 Nr. 66.

8. (103), 340ff. Nr. 67.

9. With (42), 13ff. against (103), 4.

10. (42), 73-577; (9), 40-88.

11. This concept has been modified since.

12. *é-dingira, bīt ilim*, passim, (30), 5ff.

13. *é-lugal(a)*, [8] Nr. 234 rev. II 7', also a toponym, Nr. 216 obv. II 8'-212 VI 12'.

14. *é-lú, bīt awēlim*, passim in omens [33].

15. *é-dingirata é arar Gu-aba*, "from the temple (for?) the mill of Gu-aba," [16], III, Nr. 6184 obv. 3ff.

our concept "temple" by simply using the word "house" in a context "where one is talking about gods,"[16] while describing particular temples more specifically, according to the pattern "house of the god Enlil" = "Enlil Temple."[17] The difference between "house of the god Nin-Girsu = "Nin-Girsu Temple"[18] and "so-and-so's house," that is, between a temple as we understand it and a private dwelling, lies for these peoples not in the structure but in its owner.

The floor plan of an ancient Mesopotamian temple shows that the expression "house of god" is a concrete description and not a mere metaphor like our "House of God." It is built along the lines of a dwelling,[19] hence modern architectural research has coined the terms "hearth-house," "long-room house," and "broad-room house" to characterize the different architectural types of temples.[20] For the Mesopotamian, a temple was still just a house, even when, in plan and furnishing, it far excelled all other houses. Thus even the famous step-towers,[21] which seem to have acquired their characteristic form[22] just at the time of the Third Dynasty of Ur, were still houses, to judge by their names.[23]

As language shows, temple and house are not only conceptually but functionally identical. For example, the same word is used for the "moving" by a god into a newly built or restored temple[24] and the moving into a rented house by a tenant.[25]

The Sumerian and Akkadian concept of temple, as embodied in the expression "house of a god," is thrown into relief by comparison with the corresponding concepts arrived at by other religions, peoples, and civilizations, as can be gathered from the words commonly used for "temple" in their languages—thus, for instance, *hieron*, actually "sanctuary" of the Greeks, *templum*, "reserved precinct" of the Romans, German *Kirche*, "belonging to the lord,"[26] and French *église*, "congregation,"[27] or the *mosque* of Islam, "place of prostration."[28]

Without going into its religio-historical significance, one obtains therefrom, by simple deduction, some conclusions about the nature of Babylonian temples fundamental to this inquiry. As house of a god, a temple, just like every other house, finds its natural place in a human settlement, and belongs essentially in the city, that space marked off by mankind against nature,[29] indeed originally wrested[30] from her in Babylonia. As a house the temple is of necessity housing for the god whose human fellow citizens believe him to be living there, as was explained above.

Insofar as the gods are regarded as kings,[31] to our way of thinking the temple grows to a palace[32] with an increase in the prosperity of its city, but, for the Babylonians,[33] it still falls into the category

16. (17), 171 at the right, s.v. *bītu*.
17. *é-Enlila*, passim.
18. Passim.
19. (74), 7; (80), 25 b; 27 4., compare (1), p. 21. Comparison between house and temple: (1), 1; (74), 7-10.
20. (74); (1) passim; (2), Index 226ff.
21. From the extensive literature one may mention (73); Frankfort in (10), 311; (84); (11).
22. (9), 387 with 175f.
23. This objection to be raised against (27), 53f. Compare on this also (23), 87f. to line 22.
24. *tu*, (21), 140 at the right 26 and often.
25. *erēbum*, equivalent to *tu*, (95), Nr. 139.15 and often.
26. From Greek *kyriake*.
27. From Greek *ekklesia*.
28. From Arabic *masğid* in this meaning.
29. (83), 165f.
30. (27), 51f.; (1), 3f.
31. Passim in the literature.
32. So expressly (100), 32 f) line 32; [47] Nr. 259, 2. Compare temple names like Egalmah, "Exalted Palace." Attested archaeologically by (1), 7.
33. *é-gal*, "big house," from which *ekallum* is borrowed.

"house." As a palace, the temple shelters not only the god, his family, and his divine guests, but also his servants, the priests. It contains, like a palace, great courtyards, offices, and storage rooms, kitchens, a brewery, stables and carriage houses, as Gudea of Lagash vividly describes,[34] and as excavations have brought to light.[35]

Transformation of the god's house into the god's palace brought about a change in the relationship of the temple with the populace. Whether or not in prehistoric times the house-temple, according to its layout, may have been open to the population as a whole, the temple palace of this and later periods offered enough room for a crowd of people only in the outer courts.[36] While they may have been admitted to offices and gates, they were just as rigorously excluded from the inner rooms of the temple as from the residence chambers of a royal palace.[37] Literary texts speak of a special area for festivals, apparently outside the temple where public activities took place on important holidays.[38]

How the masses conceived of the temple will probably always be unknown to us, for whatever statements are preserved on the subject in the literature are miles away from simple folk beliefs, and belong rather to the sphere of Sumerian religious poetry. Its inspired imaginings we can follow with reverent awe, albeit with scant possibilities of deep understanding,[39] in the famous cylinder inscriptions of Gudea of Lagash,[40] a high point of the art never again attained.

To the pious and learned poet the modest temple structure, on the strength of a divine fluidity resident therein, attains to a cosmic grandeur, its rather sparse rooms and cult implements lifelike reproductions or doublets of cosmic phenomena. The poet recognizes in the temple the center of his world, wherein the city god "decides" the city's "fate." He sees it humming with the activity of servant deities whose functions in the realistically conceived household of the city god and in the supernatural spheres of being are one and the same.[41] A single passage from a hymn written down in the Old Babylonian period gives a notion of this highly refined world of ideas:

> Your[42] Ekur, the holy house, the lofty abode, that is laden with awesomeness,
> Its awe-inspiring splendor reaches to heaven,
> Its shadow is spread over all lands,
> Its form stretches to the innermost reaches of heaven.[43]

From the same period we have a great cycle of poems which celebrates the temples of the principal deities in the major cult centers.[44]

The faithful may at least have heard of such lofty concepts of religious poetry in divine service. In any event, because of direct apprehension of the presence of the gods, the temple seemed to them something most sacred, surrounded with an awe-inspiring splendor of divinity to which the Babylonian instinctively offered homage as something godlike,[45] like the god's weapon, emblem, throne, vehicle, or vessel.[46] Thus we find in personal names of the widely distributed type Isidor, "gift of Isis," temples too as theophoric elements in place of the generally used gods.[47]

---

34. (29), 187f.
35. Temple complex like that of the moon god Nanna in Ur: (9), plate 401.
36. (2), 93f., in general (74), 8f.
37. In general: (76), II, 62. Attempted explanations (2), 26f.; (29), 203.
38. (36), 25 line 17; (51), 40f. line 214; 216.
39. The caution of (7), 145 is all too often overlooked.
40. (100), 88-141.
41. (64), 154; 144.
42. The god Enlil is addressed.
43. (23), 96 5.
44. (112), 245ff. with (52), 29ff.
45. *palāhu*, the word for the basic attitude of mankind toward divinity, means in general "fear something."
46. (94), 89f. 3).
47. (96), 85; 91 d.

The Role of Temples and Political History

Although the concept of temple in ancient Mesopotamian thinking is characterized by a certain consistency, so far as can be determined the reality of the temple in the public life of the First Dynasty of Babylon had a different meaning than at the time of the Third Dynasty of Ur.

If one considers it as but one facet of the relationship of society to religion, the role of the Babylonian temple during a given period was defined first and foremost by the attitude of the general public toward divinity. Reasons for changes in the relationship may be found in a modification of that attitude and lie ultimately in a shift of a society's opinions. This may be of an intellectual, moral, esthetic, or emotional nature and may be of purely psychological origin, beyond our ken. It may also be sociologically conditioned by material or political realignments or changes in the social or ethnic structure of society which, in turn, have psychological effects.

Insofar as a period of profound political, ethnic, and social upheavals followed the time of the Third Dynasty of Ur, coincidentally with change in the role of temples in Babylonian life, the one may be brought into a causal connection with the other. At any rate, a connection between the contemporaneous roles of temples and the political physiognomy of the time cannot be denied. Therefore it seems appropriate that this inquiry be divided into two sections, corresponding to these two phases of historical development, and that it treat first conditions under the Third Dynasty of Ur and thereafter those of the subsequent centuries. Since we believe that in treating our subject we have to proceed from its dependence upon and connection with historical factors, we have first to define the place of the period with which we are concerned in the over-all history of ancient Mesopotamia.

On the basis of physical remains and data obtainable from written sources, we may divide the oldest past of today's Iraq on political, cultural, religious, economic, ethnic, or linguistic grounds into three periods, more or less roughly distinguishable from each other, which may be provisionally called the prehistoric, Sumerian, and Babylonian-Assyrian periods (without attaching too much weight to such nomenclature).

Of these the time of the Third Dynasty of Ur, as the last segment of the neo-Sumerian period, represents the end of the Sumerian, or second great period of ancient Mesopotamian history.[48] The hallmark of this period is the closest connection and mutual interpenetration of society, state, and religion, to an extent perhaps unique in the history of the world. Calling this "patriarchal state socialism"[49] properly defines neither its nature nor its scope.

Ancient Sumerian social life might best be understood by comparison with a modern army in times of peace. The individual is fully integrated into the community, the purpose and goal of the organization being preservation of a society and its level of civilization. In an alluvial land carved out from ocean and swamp, ever threatened by natural disasters, and for which artificial irrigation is a prerequisite to agriculture, this is possible in the long run only through extensive collective undertakings.[50] We call such an organization a state; in the Early Dynastic period its natural environment is provided by the city, Mesopotamian antiquity's most important contribution to world history.[51]

Sumerian religion, like the state, was a collective enterprise. A major achievement of Sumerian intellect, without which perhaps monotheism might never have been thinkable, this religion created in the

---

48. The absolute dates for the more than five-hundred-year time span between the beginning of the Third Dynasty of Ur and the end of the First Dynasty of Babylon are still disputed. See most recently (107), 97 at the right and ff.; (37), 129 3. and (10), 101f.

49. (39), 178ff.

50. (27), 51f.

51. Fritz Schachermeyr, inaugural lecture at Vienna, November 20, 1952. For city-state (83), 167.

Early Dynastic period a pantheon of humanlike gods directing cosmic powers,[52] and settled them in their own cities, pride of place going to the city god as the supernatural pinnacle of the city state's organizational pyramid, then the gods of natural forces and phenomena.

Society looked after the gods resident in its midst with unceasing and often prodigious endeavors: temple buildings and gifts, cult and sacrifices. Besides metaphysical needs, the nature and extent of which remain impenetrable to us, society was evidently motivated by the conviction of the almightiness of the gods and the attendant confidence that through their service the gods can be influenced to direct, for the benefit of society, those elements of human destiny beyond the reach of mankind, such as natural events and the course of history.

Society's tireless courting of the gods, on whose benevolence its prosperity—its very existence—were thought to depend, had its origin precisely in its endeavor to ensure prosperity and existence. So much for the ancient Sumerian concepts which were still wholly viable during the Third Dynasty of Ur.

The First Dynasty of Babylon ruled toward the end of the Old Babylonian period;[53] with this commences the third and last, Babylonian-Assyrian period of ancient Mesopotamia. In broad terms, the period is marked by invasion of the civilized land by tribes of lesser culture, though linguistically related to the Akkadians; spread of the Akkadian language, founding of regional states, rivalry among petty states, feudalism, free citizenry, private enterprise, and individual religion, hence making an exact opposite to the preceding period, so far as one can use such a term in history.

The Period of the Third Dynasty of Ur

As dwellings for the powers that decide the destiny of the community, temples play their greatest role in human consciousness as the place society approaches its gods to make them merciful through service and gifts, to regain withheld or forfeited favor, and to receive their commands.[54] For this reason, the first prerequisite for orderly contact between man and god, the cult, is construction of a worthy abode for the god and equipping it for his use.[55]

The building of a big temple must have been organizationally, economically, and technically a huge undertaking for a city, such as might in some cases keep the entire social unit on the move for years. Thus, for instance, the official year of the completion of the Shara-Temple in Umma was Shu-Sin 8,[56] but the masons were already working on it in years 2, 5, and 7.[57] The laying of the foundation stone was dated as Shu-Sin 3.[58] Such a long time for construction is easily understandable, considering the size of the project.

It happens that an undated account of this time,[59] concerning the total number of bricks used for the building of the Shara-Temple at Umma and for the temple of his spouse, the goddess Nin-ara, has been preserved: 8,975,200 baked bricks and 16,832,520 smaller bricks. We learn from a small Lagash tablet of the year Amar-Sin 9,[60] shortly before the construction of the Shara-Temple, that a laborer made eighty bricks per day. The forming of the bricks alone, disregarding the baking, would require, according to this computation which is, to be sure, not the only one possible, 322,596.5 man-days; hence, for example, it would have occupied one thousand laborers for almost eleven months. And how much labor and expense were then still required just to lay the brickwork of the two temples, amounting to

52. (64), 151ff.; 138ff. II.
53. In support of this designation (55), 3.
54. For the last (29), 189ff.
55. For the Babylonian concepts (30), 5ff.
56. According to the year name Shu-Sin 9, (21), 145 85.
57. [47], Nr. 178, 176, 177.
58. (94), 75 at the left.
59. [70], 127ff.
60. [16], V, Nr. 6908.

approximately 117,000 cubic meters!

Yet the construction of the Shara-Temple was but one, and probably not one of the largest building enterprises that were completed during the reign of the Third Dynasty of Ur. Year names and building inscriptions report dozens of new constructions or reconstructions of temples.[61] Climate and the manner of construction continually required more or less comprehensive repairs of existing structures. As proud symbols of the power and wealth of the period, step towers were erected in the most important cult centers.[62]

Construction of temples was still not enough to comply with the obligation to provide worthy housing for the gods, for they also had to be properly furnished. Donors paid particular attention to objects designed for the immediate use of the gods, such as were indispensable for the cult and had to measure up to royal pretensions. For that reason, from time immemorial the finest and rarest materials were used for their manufacture: precious woods, stones, and metals imported from distant lands.[63]

Such objects included weapons and all sorts of utensils.[64] Manufacture for the more important gods of the throne,[65] bed,[66] chariot,[67] boat,[68] emblem,[69] and drum,[70] themselves considered divine, was commemorated in year names. The temples received for the gods clothing[71] and jewelry of all kinds, which were accumulated in treasuries.[72] By analogy with the following period,[73] we may also presume the production of elaborate and costly images of gods.[74]

Though inscriptions bear witness that dignitaries, officials, or members of the ruling house presented more modest gifts,[75] according to building inscriptions, year names, and other sources, temple buildings and their furnishings were exclusively the prerogative of kings.

If the benevolence of the gods was prerequisite for the well-being of the community, and service to the gods in the widest sense the way to this benevolence, then the state as an organization for the preservation of society had to view the cult as its foremost task. As surely as religion must once have been a concern for all of society, unthinkable without its intimate involvement, and remained so, it is just as certain that, from the time of our oldest recorded sources, it was also a matter of state.

The head of the old Sumerian city-state and its "government" was the city ruler.[76] Hence society's contact with the gods was primarily the task of the city ruler, who alone represented the commonality before the gods.[77] When individual cities' aspirations for hegemony, conquests, and foreign domination destroyed the political independence of the city-state and led to the unified state of the Third Dynasty of Ur, the king of Ur assumed the obligations of the city ruler, but not so much in the creation of a new imperial cult as in the maintenance of the local cults of the former city-states.

These, even as provinces, still kept their religious identity along the lines of an independent city-state. For this reason the king of Ur, like the kings of Akkad before him, was master builder of the

---

61. The survey (94), 120 is incomplete.
62. For example in Ur, Uruk, Eridu, Nippur. See note 21.
63. (100), 2f. a) V 3ff.; 66f. a) II 6-7; 68f., V 28ff.; 70f., V 53-VI 63.
64. Among many others [71] Nr. 300 and the passages cited in the following notes.
65. Amar-Sin 3, (21), 143 70; Ibbi-Sin "15," (71), 278.
66. Shulgi "15," (21), 141 33.
67. Ur-Nammu "d," (56), 397.
68. Shulgi "7," Shu-Sin 2 and 8, (21), 140 25, 144 78, and 145 84.
69. Ibbi-Sin "19," (71), 278, compare [38] Nr. 69; (32), 20 to B.22.
70. Ibbi-Sin "12," (71), 278.
71. (81), 13f.
72. [71] Nr. 702, 736, 376, 378; [47] Nr. 296.
73. Compare year names like (21), 158 171; 179 119; 180 131, etc.
74. [71] Nr. 525, 529, covering a divine image with gold? In general about this problem (74), 33ff.
75. (100), 192ff. q), r), v)-x), z), a').
76. *ensi*, in older books called *patesi* or the like.
77. (6), 35f.; (57), 300; (26a), 258f.

temples of his kingdom, unless they were erected for him as a god.[78] In either case, the costs and burdens of the enterprise were borne by the people.

When a temple was newly built or renovated, it was dedicated in a formal ceremony and the god was invested therein, as we know from the poetic account by Gudea of Lagash,[79] who probably lived in the century before the Third Dynasty of Ur, and as we may assume for later periods. The investiture was an event of importance and was commemorated in year names.[80]

The god then accepted the cult in the temple built, furnished, and dedicated to him by the king, for the pious use of the community. Cult was princely service in a double sense. It was carried on by a prince and offered to a prince. The demands of a god who was also a king were royal. It was simply a people's duty to provide for the daily meals of their ruler,[81] for, as we can see time and again, the god was thought to exist materially and all human needs were attributed to him.

Real service began only with activities that went beyond the sustenance of the god, that being taken for granted.[82] These ensued in a double cycle, monthly and yearly. Whereas the latter differed for individual gods in various cities, the monthly cycle was in principle probably more or less the same everywhere. Coordinated with the phases of the moon, and thereby identical for all months, it provided for marking the days of the first crescent, the full, and the new moon, i.e. the first, fifteenth, and twenty-eighth of the month.[83]

Among the various possibilities for further subdivision of the month,[84] one, which also treated the half lunar days as holidays, is of universal historical importance, because it seems to have become the prototype for the subdivision into weeks used by Jews and, indirectly, Christians and Moslems.[85] In the capital Ur the sacrifices were personally performed by the king, as we learn from abundant records, particularly from the time of the last king, Ibbi-Sin. These even indicate the specific types of sacrifices, kinds and quantities of things offered, their places of offering, and the time of day.[86]

The yearly cycles, beginning with the new year's festival, grouped the great and smaller festivals, some of them agricultural in origin (or so, at least their names still suggest),[87] in accordance with the monthly calendars used from time immemorial in the cities, the erstwhile city states.

As starting and finishing point for the procession of the gods, the temple was the center of festivities on holidays, in which perhaps the whole populace participated as spectators.[88] On some holidays the procession entered a special festival building outside the city, reserved for the gods and not for the public. Voyages by ship are attested, where gods visited each other from city to city.[89]

Aside from monthly and yearly celebrations, there were plenty of unforeseen circumstances when one turned spontaneously to the gods with prayers and sacrifices in the temple: cosmic calamities, such as eclipses of the sun or moon, natural catastrophes, such as failure of the Tigris to flood (which caused Gudea of Lagash to reconstruct the Nin-Girsu temple),[90] political crises, times of want, and epidemics. Yet happy events too were celebrated: thus the gods as state deities participated in the victory celebration

78. (28), 2 fifth paragraph; 27ff.; (26a), 301f. C.
79. Cylinder B, (100), 122-141.
80. See note 24.
81. (30), 5ff.
82. Concerning ancient Mesopotamian offerings and cult (5); (76), II, 81ff.
83. (60), 93-95.
84. (60), 96-99.
85. (60), 99f.
86. (58). The list can be added to.
87. (60), 22ff.
88. (30), 71f.
89. (60), 74.
90. Cylinder A I 4-9, (100), 88f.

which took place over the destruction of Shashru and Shuruthu in the year Amar-Sin 4,[91] and received as well their share of the spoils.[92]

From sources written down only later we can gain some idea of the ritual and of the liturgical literature, rich in its variety of genres, that "stream of religious lyric" which "accompanied all events of the cult";[93] nothing has come down to us from this period.

As previously mentioned, the king personally offered sacrifices in his own capital. Obviously, for practical reasons it was impossible for him to be present simultaneously in the other cities where he needed to be, as successor of the city ruler whose obligation to build temples he had in fact taken over, as we have seen. So he sent or appointed emissaries who attended the temple festivals in his stead. He traveled to important celebrations in person.[94] His expenditures for the cult were tremendous, particularly in the form of cattle for slaughter.

One might well believe that the population raised cattle only for the temple and royal palace, but not for itself. Herds, mostly of cattle and sheep, flowed in an unbroken stream from all provinces to the great shrines of the land. We have portions of the records of a stockyard called Puzrish-Dagan, grubbed out by local antiquities robbers at Drehem, near Nippur.[95] Unfortunately, the place itself has not been excavated.

Though perhaps not unique for its time, for us this stockyard stands as a unique monument of highly developed administrative centralization, state bureaucratic technique, and the consequent focusing of the whole of social life on religion. Cattle were sent there to be rerouted from the collection point to all the places they were needed. As Puzrish-Dagan served particularly the temple of nearby Nippur, but not all the other neighboring cities,[96] it can be assumed that similar distribution points existed for the other places.

Offerings by individual members of the officialdom are well attested, though quantitatively one cannot compare them with those of the king.[97]

The question may be raised as to whether the temples and their numerous functionaries were exclusively supported by the king and other lesser donors. Since that was doubtless not the case, we would like to know what the temples contributed from their own resources,[98] and how they were able to make such contributions. This can be answered only in general terms.

Ownership of land by at least the most important temples, attested for earlier periods, may have continued, and cultivation of such land brought in a return. Herds and treasures could be accumulated by contributions from members of the royal household and functionaries,[99] though not from private individuals, as these were unknown in this period. Slaves acquired by donation or as spoils of war may have constituted a work force for internal use, or for hire.[100]

That temples really had their own income is corroborated not just directly by innumerable documents, but also indirectly by well known cases of payments by temples to "the palace," i.e. to the government.[101] Such payments are but one example of the statism of the epoch, difficult to describe, which can only be understood as a whole, because it included all aspects of public and private life. Its far-flung and painstakingly precise administration has left us imposing remains of its bookkeeping.

---

91. (92) (c), 81f.
92. (81), 19 note 43.
93. (64), 155.
94. (60), 26.
95. (101), 186.
96. (94), 54 at the left, 397, end.
97. (92) (c), 60ff.
98. (92) (c), 76 4-81.
99. (92) (b), 7 A.RU.A 4), first citation (from RA 17, 209).
100. (81), 19 note 43; 68 G7 note b.
101. [43] Nr. 112 115, 117-120, 122, 124, 126.

No period of ancient Mesopotamian history has left us nearly so many written documents as that of the Third Dynasty of Ur. Not counting royal inscriptions, approximately fifteen thousand[102] legal and administrative documents have so far been published one way or another, mostly official transactions and relatively fewer business and juridical records.[103] Many times more than this must still be unpublished. The tablets come primarily from ancient sites such as Lagash, Umma, Puzrish-Dagan, Nippur, and Ur in south and central Babylonia and contain a great variety of information about temples and cults.

The remarkable fact that Assyriology has not yet succeeded in exploring thoroughly the civilization of this period, despite such a wealth of data,[104] should not be passed over without a brief explanation. On one hand, the vast bulk of the sources and the unanswered questions as to how they might be mastered stands precisely in the way of exploiting them;[105] on the other, they mostly came from illegal excavations or thievery and thereby arrived on the antiquities market, thence to be scattered—more than any other type of tablet—to countless museums and private collections over the entire world.

Added to the material difficulties of mastering what is available are difficulties of language and subject matter. The philologist is confronted with official notations phrased mostly in laconic brevity, often set out as registers, personnel rosters, or tables, and which, accordingly, give us or let us guess no more information about what interests us than a modern streetcar ticket furnishes about generation of electric current or a postage stamp about the organization of the postal system. He is also confronted by hundreds and thousands of words[106] which, often as not, still remain lifeless vocables to him even if he knows their literal meanings, because he has no perception of the things and events they signify.

It is worth noting in this context that the available efforts toward a presentation of the civilization[107] of this period mostly date to the time a beginning was being made and one had to contend with fewer documents, and that the burgeoning of the material at hand has evidently frustrated further attempts.

For all these reasons nothing certain can be said concerning what certain role temples must have played as economic and social factors thanks to their possessions, though one is usually inclined to make it a very important one. This is because the many known details cannot be fitted together into a cohesive picture, and most of all because their scope and proportionality to recognizable phenomena remain undemonstrable.

One widely spread, fundamental misconception is certainly to be combatted, though, even if that results only in negative certainty: the records in question are not, by and large, "temple records," as has been unjustifiably assumed since their first discovery and even expressed in the titles of books.[108] They were not even demonstrably found in "temple archives."[109] Impartial consideration shows clearly that these were public records, that is, of the central state or city authorities.

Frequent mention of temples and their affairs can be explained on the one hand by the above-mentioned mutual dependency of all branches of public life in a statist system which, in terms of its extent and longevity, was perhaps the most important of its kind in antiquity, and, on the other, by the outstanding significance of temples for the state and community, whence the importance attached to their

102. The number has increased considerably since this was written.

103. See the careful bibliography (81), 215-224, with more than 12,300 texts until 1948, to which the 393 numbers in the book itself may be added. [71] with 1802 texts is not included. Publications continue to appear, (46), etc.

104. (81), VII; (92) (a), 1-9.

105. For the problem in general (34).

106. (81), 225-260; (71), 47-192.

107. (66), (32): 1911; (69): 1912; (12): 1915.

108. [4], [89], [67], [47], [38]: 1896-1937.

109. One encounters this assumption in the first instance for the tablets from Lagash (98), 118, although (40), 65-67 communicates nothing about the findspot. As at Umma, it is not established. The "temple archive" of Nippur is treated as an established fact in (41), 28ff., (42), 248ff. Yet even if the archives from Nippur and Ur were housed on temple property, that does not prove that they were "temple archives." Note as a typical example the table of contents of (78), 18-20, in which among the 171 published "temple documents" only four turn out to be "special temple accounts," p. 20.

interests in public affairs. From this it becomes clear that much of what, in certain modern presentations, has been attributed to temples on the basis of preconceived opinion does not pertain to them at all, but to the state administration of the Third Dynasty of Ur. So, for example, the stockyard at Puzrish-Dagan touched upon earlier was not a dependency of the Enlil-temple of Nippur, as has been assumed, but a state institution that provided the royal court too with cattle.[110]

In spite of all available details, much less is known about the human component of the temple institution, the temple personnel,[111] than would be required for accurate insight into their situation. This rather open-ended term "personnel" should refer primarily—and then only with respect to larger temples—to the presumably considerable number of people who lived for and from the temples, and, in a wider sense, perhaps, even in the temples. These were by no means only priests, for when temples had extensive possessions and worked them themselves, there is a strong numerical preponderance of workers, foremen, technical staff, and administrative personnel[112] under the direction of a temple manager and his assistant.[113]

Neither Sumerian nor Akkadian has a generic term "priest"; only modern scholarship combines under that name a whole series of designations of status. The individual categories of so-called priests had clearly differentiated ranks and functions. Among the people who belong to the temple in its capacity as a religious institution we can distinguish actual priests, concerned with the cult in all its forms,[114] from the female personnel, about whom little is known. Some of them had personal connections with the king.[115]

Quite apart from and above the temple personnel are the "god's lord" and the "god's lady," at least some of them of royal descent,[116] with their own residence and staff,[117] and apparently with only little contact with the temple, though close ties to the deity.[118] Only for them is it accurate to say that during the time of the Third Dynasty of Ur and the subsequent periods[119] did the king appoint priests. The election and investiture of the "god's lord" and the "god's lady" were matters of state commemorated in year names.[120]

Even less can be determined about the social role of temples as the seat or gathering place of temple personnel, because this personnel, as has been explained above, was not uniform either socially or professionally. One has only an impression that they had developed their own independent existence and did not appear in public life so much as in, for example, the Early Dynastic period, when temple functionaries were important personages in the public life of the city state, or in the subsequent period when the gods and the priests with them went out among the people.[121]

As exponents of state and society, temples, deified and exalted in literature to the high heavens, the objects of unceasing efforts of the ruler and the people, shared their destiny with them. They became rich or poor, towered to the skies, or fell into ruins, as the esteemed genre of lamentations over the destruction of cities and temples so vividly portrays for us.[122]

---

110. [69] Nr. 59. 280f., 284; [93] Nr. 23 obv. 1-4.
111. In the meantime intensive study has been devoted to the matter.
112. (14).
113. (92) (d), 73-83 III and IV; (15) Nr. 314, 28; 295ff., 1.
114. (92) (d), 87ff. VII, in addition *išib*, *gala*, *nar*, etc., concerning which in general (76), II, 64ff.
115. (79), 23; (86); compare (24).
116. (62), 129.
117. (100), 198ff. 2), i). Accounts [43] Nr. 1, [48], 20-23. Compare (94), 2 at the right, f).
118. (92) (d), 83-87 V and VI.
119. (76), II, 60, (57), 202.
120. Ur-Nammu "b," (21), 140 16; "f," (56), 398; Shulgi, (21), 141 32, 34, 47; 142 62; Amar-Sin, (21), 143 71f., 144 75f.; Ibbi-Sin, (21), 145 87; (71), 278 23.
121. (30), 64ff.
122. (51).

Documents from the end of this period, when the power of the dynasty was going downhill, and when Ibbi-Sin, its last representative, was confined to his capital, show the abandonment of sacrifices, apparently on account of the difficult economic situation of the state and the shrinkage of the cult.[123] The temples of Ur, showered with presents by kings for nearly a century, finally served, if the comparison may be made, as piggy banks to be emptied in times of need, as they yielded gold and silver, copper, and bronze "or the buying off of Isin,"[124] this for the sake of the state whose very existence was threatened, and with which they were bound, for better or worse.[125]

In the meantime, the ancient Sumerian shrine of the god Enlil at Nippur, having fallen into the hands of the ascendant king of Isin[126] had already officially acknowledged that dangerous and finally victorious rival of the last king of Ur. With this begins a new phase in the political history of the land as well as in the development of the position of the Babylonian temples.

The Old Babylonian Period

Royal inscriptions and year names of the Old Babylonian period clearly indicate that, in the numerous successor states of the Neo-Sumerian empire of the Third Dynasty of Ur, rulers' efforts to maintain the temples were by no means diminished. In lands large and small the tradition continues of considerable temple construction and of almost inconceivable quantities of donations of cult objects and dedicatory offerings.[127] Yet, as in other phases of life, here too much seems to have changed in comparison to the situation under the Third Dynasty of Ur.

Although despite the ample building activities, Old Babylonian temples do not measure up to those of the preceding period, so far as is known from excavations—many constructions seem only to be renovations of temple constructions of the kings of Ur[128]—this need not be given overmuch weight, for on one hand one always has to be cautious that the accidental results of excavation may have created a false impression, or, on the other hand, if discoveries indeed reflect the true state of affairs, one might seek to explain this by the often undeniable constriction of the new economic situation.

In fact, the change lies rather in the different concept of the temple, as it is no longer seen in this period as the locus of contact with the gods, so essential to the life of the community, nor as guarantor of the collective existence. Taking into account that the thoughts and feelings of those people were buried with them, and that we must satisfy ourselves with the literature, be it religious poetry, be it official writings, a mere shadow of the vital spirit, we will not expect to find this proposed change of conception clearly expressed in the texts available to us.

Literature, and particularly religious and official literature, is conservative and loath to give up prior formulation. Even when its meaning for contemporaneous usage has been lost and its emotional impact dulled, it is retained as esteemed phraseology, old and familiar, guarded as a proper, even indispensible appurtenance. Thus this literature, and not just in Babylon, is behind the spirit of the times, if not in outright tendentious opposition to it, knowingly denying or seeking to deny its developments. Not what literature solemnly repeats from hoary tradition, but the novelty that it sometimes lets slip through, this is what gives us a glimpse of the real sentiment of its time.

If one reads the lengthy self-praise of Hammurabi in the celebrated stela inscription with the laws

---

123. With permission of Professor Thorkild Jacobsen, Chicago, taken from the manuscript of his review of (71), kindly made available by him.

124. (26), 42 at the right.

125. [71] Nr. 702.

126. (25), 62 line 15ff. with p. 74.

127. Besides among the numerous royal inscriptions, especially in year names, Isin: (21), 147 at the right—148 at the right, 184 at the right, 256; (87), 129f.; (13), 16f.; (55), 4-9; (97), 48f; Eshnunna: (28), 170-195; Larsa: (21), 155 at the right—164 at the left; Babylon: (21), 174 at the right—192 at the left. For the smaller states, among others, (21), 192ff.

128. Ur: (9), 78ff.; Uruk: (44), 24ff., (45), 9.

of that king,[129] and if one accepts the interpretation presented here whereby the kings of the period of the Ur III Dynasty were heirs and legitimate successors to the former city rulers within the empire, then one might expect to find Hammurabi portrayed here in that same way. But a closer look shows important differences.

Now it is the king himself who takes care of the ancient cities, no longer the city god, though, to be sure, the latter is usually mentioned as well. We find this idea in the pronouncements of other rulers of that time,[130] but in earlier periods only once: in the inscription of the conqueror Lugalzagesi from the end of the Early Dynastic period.[131] Furthermore, temples now cited by their own name appear after or alongside their cities[132] as independent objects of royal concern. Rulers now describe themselves as protectors of and providers for specifically named temples.[133] This can only mean that the ancient unity of city and temple had been dissolved, or at least loosened, and that temples were felt to be separate entities within and apart from the city.

We will never be able to follow this development in all its phases through the centuries of the Old Babylonian period and the patchwork of lands, large and small, enduring and ephemeral in their power. Yet surely a close relationship between it and political happenstance may be suggested.

This development may be explained by the disappearance of the earlier city states, which, under the rule of the Third Dynasty of Ur, had still existed at least as provinces, invasion by foreign tribes, and the emergence of territorial states. But the decisive factor in this development was the formation of a new society of free men, yeomen and small tenants on state lands, loosely connected to the state as subjects of the king,[134] with a new individual religious feeling that brought the individual into a direct relationship with the gods.[135]

If the community, defined socially and religiously as the sum of individuals with personal religious convictions, did not need the temple any more for its direct approach to the deity, so too temples for their part participated as economic and social organisms in the same process of emancipation from the all-encompassing state that was taking place in society. Temples, concretely expressed, became property owners along with other property owners, entrepreneurs, and taxpayers in company with other entrepreneurs and taxpayers; priests and temple personnel became professionals like other professionals.

The starting point of our essay was that kings were the particular patrons of temples. Construction of a temple by a private citizen,[136] attested by a document, certainly throws a clear light on the changed religious feeling of the time and on the new position of the temple in society, but this remains a unique instance. If the large temples, though on a materially reduced scale, continued their cults in inherited forms for the common good, that happened not for reasons of tradition alone but manifestly at the wish and behest, and hence the expense, of the king.[137]

While official religion had always been a matter of state in Mesopotamia, now it is explicitly a matter of government. Beginning with the Old Babylonian period we can rightfully speak of an alliance between throne and altar; but now ruler and temple are no longer integral parts of a city state constituted as a closed whole, but are independent entities within a system of factors bound together by a whole

---

129. I 27 - V 13. Most recent translation (88), 163-180. For the passage (20), xxviiiff.

130. For the title "who cares for the city X" (100), 206 5 line 2, 209 5. I 3, 212 b) I 5, 216 a) line 13, and epithets ibidem lines 11-15.

131. (100), 154f. II 26-III 2.

132. In eighteen of twenty-four examples.

133. (100), 222 c) line 8; 212 I 7ff., 216 a) line 14, 17. Such titles have nothing to do with the older "builder of the temple X," p. 164 2. a) line 2f.

134. For the social position of the people called *muškēnum*, whom one assumes to be persons of less than full rights of citizenship, evidence is still lacking. (102), 1ff.

135. (96), 72, (64), 155 and 144f. IV, (30), 66.

136. (95) Nr. 220.

137. (57), 207 with note 34, (104) Nr. 9 lines 11-13; 80.

network of interconnected relationships, the end result of which we call the territorial state.

The kings who now openly asked the gods for a stable government, a firmly established throne, and obedience from their subjects,[138] needed religious sanction more than ever. Their very first act of state, the coronation, took place in the temple where the royal insignia were kept.[139] One of the rivals of Samsuiluna of Babylon, the "pretender" Rim-Sin, explicitly has himself elevated to kingship by the goddess Ninmah in the temple of Kesh.[140] In the further course of their reigns rulers regularly fulfilled their cultic obligations in the temple, starting on new year's day, as can be assumed from their lavish outlays for the temple on the occasion of this festival.[141]

If kings want the temples' support, they have every reason not only to put their priesthood in their debt, but also to promote the institutions as such and to maintain their prestige. Thus we find temples enjoying royal privileges, even such prerogatives as the king himself possessed. The Code of Hammurabi puts theft of "possessions of the gods" on the same level as theft of royal possessions and imposes on both kinds of theft harsh punishment.[142]

For the benefit of particularly important temples, rulers seem to have abrogated taxation in their cities, as can be deduced from one of the year names of the king Ur-Ninurta of Isin.[143] In addition, the "liberation" of the inhabitants of his principal cities, which Lipit-Ishtar of Isin attributes to himself,[144] could also have had that meaning. The Shamash temple in Sippar may have claimed similar favors, invoking with a forged document the privileges of a king of Akkad who liberated numerous localities "for Shamash" and "did not require labor service of them"; thereafter "they performed labor service for the god."[145]

The practical consequence of such abrogation by kings of the right to collect taxes or to call up for labor service are not known. Nor do we know if we should see in them actual donations or rather a sort of abdication of responsibilities such as the cost of sacrifices and cult. Transfer of real estate in such a case is now shown, at least for Assyria, by a newly found inscription where king Irishum "cedes" to the god Assur a number of parcels of real estate in his capital Assur.[146] No general statements can be made about the land held by temples or its administration. Some at least of the main temples of this period must have had extensive lands and considerable economic potential.[147]

Priests and temple personnel, like the temples, came to adapt themselves to the new social and economic conditions. At any rate, the numerous and elaborately structured priesthood seems to have occupied[148] a respected and economically advantageous position among the class of free citizens, as is shown by a great number of business documents of the time.[149] The material circumstances of these priests and temple personnel were characterized by possession of temple offices of precisely measurable worth, which could be inherited or alienated like real estate, and endowed besides with fixed benefits and often substantial incomes.[150]

There is documentation regarding a peculiar institution of this period, a kind of endowed foundation

---

138. (100), 208f. 5. a) II 16-18, 214f. d) rev. 16-18, 216f. f) II 10ff., 220f. e) II 9ff. Already somewhat similar, Gudea of Lagash, Statue E VIII 2f., (59), 84f.

139. [85] Nr. 76 rev. VII, partially translated by Jacobsen (26a), 245ff.

140. (21), 164 283.

141. Year name Samsuiluna 27, (21), 184 172.

142. §6; 8.

143. (55), 5 (b).

144. (88), 159 at the right.

145. [49], 2 IV 27-V 14. Concerning the nature of the so-called "cruciform monument," most recently (31), 347f.

146. (65), 224f. lines 8-11 with pp. 235-237 d).

147. [35].

148. (55), 155f.

149. (95), (50), III-VI.

150. (76), II, 58.

for women annexed to a temple. One of these has been excavated.[151] Its members belong mostly to the affluent citizenry. Though the title or rank "canoness" can be documented from the end of the Early Dynastic period[152] and from the time of the Dynasty of Akkad,[153] and the institution of such a foundation is attested from the time of the Third Dynasty of Ur,[154] only now in this period do foundations, perhaps through a sort of gentrification, become socially important. This is shown by the consideration afforded them in the so-called Code of Lipit-Ishtar[155] and in the Code of Hammurabi,[156] which contain as well regulations for "ladies of the god"[157] and other classes of women[158] connected with the temple. In Sippar, the canonesses ultimately dominated the economic life of the city.[159]

As the needs of the public had changed, a substantial number of clerics no longer exercised their responsibilities in the temple proper, especially the incantation priests and soothsayers, who instead called on their clients. The immense spread of haruspicy and its indispensability for all state undertakings[160] entailed that even military units on the march be accompanied by haruspices, just as later soldiers would be by their field chaplains.[161]

From the requirements of civic life new functions accrued to the temple, for which its religious character and economic status rendered it qualified as one of the constituent elements of public life. Its unique importance in the legal activity of the time was based on its quality of being the highest instance of moral appeal. On the one hand, the temple could guarantee utmost honesty and permanence of human arrangements by divine sanction, and in doing so offered an important, frequently utilized service to a society that strove by all possible means to lend validity and permanence to its numerous civil contractual relationships. On the other hand, the temple could, when needful, arouse the human conscience as no other power could. Rendering palpable and impressive the awesomeness of the divine, the temple appealed to fear of the gods, their omnipotence, and power to punish, and thus preserved man from falsehood and led him into truth.

In earlier periods temples had already penetrated everyday affairs through one path or another, generally with the same justification based on the Babylonians' fear of the gods. But the enormous increase in commerce and the disputes and lawsuits resulting from it and from increased private property and greater personal freedom, led to such a broadening and differentiation of temple activity in the juridical sphere as had never before taken place.

Whereas, from of old, contracts of all kinds had been sworn to in the name of the king,[162] a practice maintained unchanged only in Nippur,[163] in most places there is now added oath by the city god and eventually the god of the land.[164] Actually, these oaths may not always have been taken in temples,[165] nor is there proof that all legal documents were deposited in temples, as proposed by some authors.[166] However, drawing up of lease, rental, and loan contracts in the presence of the gods is

---

151. (91), 21-29.
152. [99] Nr. 61 X 1.
153. (77) Nr. 179. For [49], 1 III 28, 2 IV 8 see (31).
154. [71] Nr. 1001 line 12.
155. §22. Most recent translation (88), 159-161.
156. §110, 144-147, 178-182.
157. §22-§110, 178f.
158. §22-§178-181, 183f., 187, 192f.
159. (68), 118f., 121, (95), 67.
160. (30), 54.
161. (30), 77 with note 1.
162. (55), 107 (g). In general, for the oath, also the following, (21), 305ff.
163. (55), 97 with note 19.
164. (75), 49ff., (20), 466 (VI).
165. (106), 195.
166. (55), 124.

attested.[167] Accountings of inheritance and commercial ventures likewise took place in temples,[168] as well as the formal manumission of slaves.[169]

The role of the temple in juridical proceedings has been misunderstood, as if there had existed an earlier "temple jurisdiction" that was gradually displaced by a "civil jurisdiction."[170] In fact, even the preceding Neo-Sumerian period knows of no temple court, only administering an oath in the temple to one of the parties.[171] A court resorts to the oath as a means of reaching the truth only when objective means, testimony of witnesses and documentation, turn out to be insufficient.[172] In such cases the plaintiff has to swear an assertory oath[173] and the defendant an oath of clearance,[174] the assertory portion of which transcribes exactly the court's findings.[175] The laws of Eshnunna[176] and the Hammurabi Code adduce such cases,[177] not all of which need have been matters of litigation.

The Neo-Sumerian period already knows the declaratory or exculpatory oath in questions of fact, such as arise in §266,[178] and which seems to reflect official administrative practice. The court refers the parties to the temple for execution of an oath, just as today religious oaths are required and taken for secular purposes.[179] A second way temples established truth, determination of contested boundaries by the use of divine symbols on the spot,[180] is still obscure.

At any rate, temples were called in by the civil judiciary only because of their power over souls, when they sent a party or sometimes the witnesses to the awesome place of oath-taking, psychologically a moment of the greatest significance, in order to bestow the ultimate validity of a divine verdict upon a judgment which the court had already reached but could not prove. For us, though perhaps not for the Babylonians, this is radically different from divine judgment or the ordeal,[181] which had in fact been provided for in certain rare instances in Hammurabi's code,[182] but contrary to earlier[183] and later[184] periods is so far not attested in Babylonia itself for the Old Babylonian period.[185] But even the participation of temples in establishing truth recedes with the passing of time, the situation to which the aforementioned modern view of the "emergence of a civil judiciary" refers.

The most specific proof for the adaptability of temples to changing circumstances is their important role in the economy as banking institutions, especially as played by temples of the sun god Shamash.[186] They granted loans to people, sometimes without interest,[187] and used their wealth for their own and

---

167. (106), 195.
168. (106), 210, (63), 76f. 6 I 20ff.
169. (106), 212.
170. (106), 180ff. That the hypothesis is unsustainable follows from Walther's cautious statements and by the following.
171. [99] Nr. 295 obv. 10ff.
172. (106), 223.
173. An example (55), 164ff.
174. (106), 226.
175. (55), 193.
176. §37. Most recent translation (88), 161-163.
177. §9, 23, 98, 106f., 120, 126, 240, 266, 281.
178. [16], V Nr. 6913 rev. 1f., 8231 obv. 4f.
179. For the corresponding documentary entries (55), 58ff. with correction p. 225.
180. (106) 200ff.
181. (19), 86ff.
182. §2, 32, for which see (20), 62ff., 284.
183. (22), 335.
184. See note 181.
185. The case cited in (20), 64 comes about by order of the king of the non-Babylonian city of Carchemish on the middle Euphrates.
186. (95), 71 d.
187. (95), 67.

community benefit. A certain social concern is in this instance undeniable.[188] These transactions must have been numerous, as is shown by frequent mention[189] of the "interest rate of Shamash" being the norm, and the "*seah*-measures of Shamash or Marduk."[190] As was mentioned above, the Shamash canonesses also granted loans.

The financially secure position of the temples, their continuous availability of cash, and their social mission can explain the provision in the Code of Hammurabi[191] whereby Babylonian prisoners of war who had been bought by slave traders in foreign countries and then brought back home should be redeemed by the temple of their place of residence if the necessary money could not be found otherwise. An actual royal order to this effect has been preserved.[192]

The temple has also been viewed in Assyriology as the center of cultivation of the literature which dates mainly from this period or was then fixed in writing. In fact, tablets with literary texts are attested "in the temple" from the later Seleucid period on,[193] though the once-notorious controversy over the existence of a "temple library of Nippur" has since been decided in the negative.[194] The literary texts transmitted to us may rather have come from palaces and schools.[195]

Regarding the latter, some of which are thought to have been excavated,[196] we now know with certainty that they had nothing to do with temples.[197] A charming little essay about life in school, the only known realistic portrayal of daily life in Babylonia, shows this to have been a secular private institution, the students of which had to pay tuition to a strict task master.[198]

Even without promoting justice or spreading culture, the temple, in its traditional and newly undertaken tasks, played a vital role in the public life of the Old Babylonian period and continued to do so as long as there were Babylonians.

188. (61), 27.
189. (63), 17 2 I 16f., (95), 66 a).
190. (63), 34f., 3 I 27-31.
191. §32.
192. (68), 6f.
193. (88), 342 sub f.
194. (108), 140 at the right, (109), 134 at the left.
195. (34), 102 on rooms 108, 115.
196. (54), 245.
197. (64), 155f. and 146.
198. (53).

BIBLIOGRAPHY

1. Walter Andrae, *Das Gotteshaus und die Urformen des Bauens im alten Orient* (Berlin: Hans Schoetz & Co., 1930).
2. — *Das wiedererstandene Assur* (Leipzig: J. C. Hinrichs, 1938).
3. *Archiv für Orientforschung, internationale Zeitschrift für die Wissenschaft vom Vorderen Orient*, herausgegeben von Ernst (F.) Weidner (Band 3-13 Berlin, 14 Berlin-Graz, from 15 on Graz: Selbstverlag des Herausgebers, 1926 ff.).
4. Will.-R. Arnold, *Ancient Babylonian Temple Records in the Columbia University Library* (New York: 1896).
5. F. Blome, *Die Opfermaterie in Babylonien und Israel*, I. Teil (Rome: Pontificio Istituto Biblico, 1934).
6. Franz M. Th. Böhl, *Der babylonische Fürstenspiegel*: Mitteilungen der Altorientalischen Gesellschaft, XI, 3 (Leipzig: Otto Harrassowitz, 1937).
7. Jacob Burckhardt, *Weltgeschichtliche Betrachtungen* (Leipzig: Alfred Kröner, n.d.).
8. Edward Chiera, Sumerian Lexical Texts from the Temple School of Nippur: (105), Vol. XI (1929).
9. Viktor Christian, *Altertumskunde des Zweistromlandes von der Vorzeit bis zum Ende der Achämenidenherrschaft* (Leipzig: Karl W. Hiersemann, 1940).
10. *Compte Rendu de la Seconde Rencontre Assyriologique internationale, organisée à Paris du 2 au 6 juillet 1951 par le Groupe François Thureau-Dangin* (Paris: Imprimerie Nationale, 1951).
11. *Comptes Rendus de la Première Rencontre Assyriologique internationale Paris 26-28 juin 1950* (Leiden: E. J. Brill, 1951).
12. G. Contenau, *Contribution à l'histoire économique d'Umma*: Bibliothèque de l'Ecole des Hautes Etudes, 219e fascicule (Paris: Librairie Ancienne Honoré Champion, 1915).
13. Vaughn E. Crawford, "An Ishbī-Irra Date Formula," (46), II, 1948, 13-19.
14. Anton Deimel, "Die Rangordnung unter den Tempelverwaltern in Lagaš zur Zeit der Könige von Ur," *Mitteilungen der Vorderasiatischen Gesellschaft*, 21 (1917), 226-32.
15. — Šumerisches Lexikon (Rome: Pontificio Istituto Biblico, 1925 ff.).
16. L. Delaporte, Henri de Genouillac, and Fr. Thureau-Dangin, *Mission Française de Chaldée. Inventaire des tablettes de Tello conservées au Musée Impérial Ottoman* (Paris: Ernest Leroux, 1910-1921).
17. Friedrich Delitzsch, *Assyrisches Handwörterbuch* (Leipzig: J. C. Hinrichs, 1896).
18. Pinhas Delougaz and Seton Lloyd, *Pre-Sargonid Temples in the Diyala Region*: (105), LVIII (1942).
19. G. R. Driver and John C. Miles, *The Assyrian Laws Edited with Translation and Commentary* (Oxford: Clarendon Press, 1935).
20. — *The Babylonian Laws Edited with Translation and Commentary*, I (Oxford: Clarendon Press, 1952).
21. Erich Ebeling and Bruno Meissner (Herausgeber): *Reallexikon der Assyriologie* (Berlin and Leipzig: Walter de Gruyter & Co., 1928-1938) — (citation in volume II).
22. A. Falkenstein, "Eine gesiegelte Tontafel der altsumerischen Zeit," (3), XIV (1941-1944), 333-36.
23. — "Untersuchungen zur sumerischen Grammatik (Fortsetzung)," (111), XLVIII (1944), 69-118.
24. — "Eine Hymne auf Šūsîn von Ur," *Die Welt des Orients*, Heft 2 (1947), 43-50.
25. — "Ibbīsîn-Išbi'erra," (111), XLIX (1950), 59-79.
26. — Besprechung von (71), *Journal of the American Oriental Society*, 72 (1952), 40-45.

26a. Henri Frankfort, *Kingship and the Gods: A Study of Ancient Near Eastern Religion as the Integration of Society and Nature* (Chicago: University of Chicago Press, 1948).
27. — *The Birth of Civilization in the Near East* (London: Williams & Norgate, Ltd., 1951).
28. —, Seton Lloyd and Thorkild Jacobsen, *The Gimilsin Temple and the Palace of the Rulers at Tell Asmar*: (105), XLIII (1940).
29. H. and H. A. Frankfort, John A. Wilson, Th. Jacobsen, and William A. Irwin, *The Intellectual Adventure of Ancient Man: An Essay on Speculative Thought in the Ancient Near East* (Chicago: University of Chicago Press, 1946).
30. C. J. Gadd, *Ideas of Divine Rule in the Ancient East: The Schweich Lectures of the British Academy, 1945.* (London: Geoffrey Cumberlege, Oxford University Press, 1948).
31. I. J. Gelb, "The Date of the Cruciform Monument of Maništušu," *Journal of Near Eastern Studies*, VIII (1949), 346-48.
32. H. de Genouillac, *La trouvaille de Dréhem: Etude avec un choix de textes de Constantinople et Bruxelles* (Paris: Paul Geuthner, 1911).
33. Albrecht Goetze, *Old Babylonian Omen Texts*: (110), X (1947).
34. G. Goossens, "Introduction à l'archivéconomie de l'Asie antérieure," (90), XLVI (1952), 98-107.
35. Ettalene Mears Grice, *Records from Ur and Larsa Dated in the Larsa Dynasty*: (110), V (1919).
36. Hans-Gustav Güterbock, "Die historische Tradition und ihre literarische Gestaltung bei Babyloniern und Hethitern bis 1200," (111), XLII (1934), 1-91.
37. — "Türkische Beiträge zum Studium des Alten Orients," (3), XV (1945-1951), 128-35.
38. George Gottlob Hackman, *Temple Documents of the Third Dynasty of Ur from Umma: Babylonian Inscriptions in the Collection of James B. Nies, Yale University*, V (New Haven: Yale University Press, 1937).
39. Fritz M. Heichelheim, *Wirtschaftsgeschichte des Altertums*, I (Leiden: Sijthoff, 1938).
40. Léon Heuzey, "Mission de M. de Sarzec en Chaldée: Huitième campagne de fouilles (1894)," (90), III (1894), 65-67.
41. H. V. Hilprecht, *Old Babylonian Inscriptions Chiefly from Nippur*, II (Philadelphia: reprint from the Transactions of the American Philosophical Society, N.S., Vol. XVIII, No. 3, 1896).
42. — *The Excavations in Assyria and Babylonia* (Philadelphia: A. J. Holman & Co., 1904).
43. Mary Inda Hussey, *Sumerian Tablets in the Harvard Semitic Museum, Part II: From the Time of the Dynasty of Ur*: Harvard Semitic Series, IV (Cambridge, Mass.: Harvard University Press, 1915).
44. Julius Jordan, *Erster vorläufiger Bericht über die von der Notgemeinschaft der deutschen Wissenschaft in Uruk-Warka unternommenen Ausgrabungen.* Aus den Abhandlungen der Preussischen Akademie der Wissenschaften Jahrgang 1929. Phil.-hist. Klasse No. 7 (Berlin: Verlag der Akademie der Wissenschaften, 1930).
45. — *Zweiter Vorläufiger Bericht über die von der Notgemeinschaft der deutschen Wissenschaft in Uruk unternommenen Ausgrabungen* (cf. Note 44, 1930) — No. 4 (cf. Note 44, 1931).
46. *Journal of Cuneiform Studies*, edited by Albrecht Goetze, Yale University, Thorkild Jacobsen, University of Chicago, and Abraham Sachs, Brown University (New Haven: The American Schools of Oriental Research, 1947 ff.).
47. Clarence Elwood Keiser, *Selected Temple Documents of the Ur Dynasty*: (110), IV (1919).
48. (Leonard) W. King, *Cuneiform Texts from Babylonian Tablets, &c.*, in *The British Museum*, X (London: The British Museum, 1900).
49. — — XXXII (1912).
50. J. Kohler, P. Koschaker, and A. Ungnad, *Hammurabi's Gesetz*, II-VI (Leipzig: Eduard Pfeiffer, 1909-1923).
51. Samuel Noah Kramer, *Lamentation over the Destruction of Ur*, The Oriental Institute of the University of Chicago, Assyriological Studies, 12 (Chicago: University of Chicago Press, 1940).
52. — *Sumerian Literary Texts from Nippur in the Museum of the Ancient Orient at Istanbul*: The Annual of the American Schools of Oriental Research, XXII (cf. No. 46, 1944).
53. — "Schooldays: A Sumerian Composition Relating to the Education of a Scribe," *Journal of the American Oriental Society*, LXIX (1949), 199-215.
54. — "The Sumerian School: A pre-Greek System of Education," *Studies Presented to David Moore Robinson* (St. Louis: 1951).
55. F. R. Kraus, *Nippur und Isin nach altbabylonischen Rechtsurkunden*: (46), III (1951).
56. — "Zur Chronologie der Könige Ur-Nammu und Šulgi von Ur," *Orientalia*, N.S., XX (1951), 385-98.

57. René Labat, *Le caractère religieux de la royauté assyro-babylonienne* (Paris: Adrien Maisonneuve, 1939).
58. Maurice Lambert, "Nouveaux documents concernant la ville d'Ur," (90), XLIV (1950), 73-87.
59. — and J.-R. Tournay, "Les statues D, G, E et H de Gudéa (Textes concernant la déesse Bau)," (90), XLVI (1952), 75-86.
60. Benno Landsberger, *Der kultische Kalender der Babylonier und Assyrer*: (72), VI, 142 (1915).
61. — "Solidarhaftung von Schuldnern in den babyl.-assyrischen Urkunden," (111), XXXV (1924), 22-36.
62. — Besprechung von Gadd und Legrain, Ur excavations, Texts I, *Orientalistische Literaturzeitung*, 1931, 115-36.
63. — *Die Serie ana ittišu*: Materialien zum sumerischen Lexikon I (Rome: Pontificio Istituto Biblico, 1937).
64. — "Die geistigen Leistungen der Sumerer," *Ankara Üniversitesi Dil ve Tarih-Coğrafya Fakültesi Dergisi*, III (1945), 137-58.
65. — and K. Balkan, "Die Inschrift des assyrischen Königs Irišum, gefunden in Kültepe 1948," *Belleten*, XIV (1950), 219-68.
66. Stephen Langdon, *Tablets from the Archives of Drehem with a Complete Account of the Origin of the Sumerian Calendar, Translation, Commentary, and 23 plates* (Paris: Paul Geuthner, 1911).
67. Robert Julius Lau, *Old Babylonian Temple Records*: Columbia University Oriental Studies, III (New York: Columbia University Press, 1906).
68. W. F. Leemans, *The Old-Babylonian Merchant, his Business and his Social Position*: Studia et documenta ad iura orientis antiqui pertinentia, III (Leiden: E. J. Brill, 1950).
69. Léon Legrain, *Le temps des rois d'Ur: Recherches sur la société antique d'après des textes nouveaux*: cf. No. 12, 119e fascicule (1912).
70. — "Quelques textes anciens," (90), XXXII (1933), 125-1.
71. — *Business Documents of the Third Dynasty of Ur: Ur Excavations*, Texts, III (London and Philadelphia: 1937-1947).
72. *Leipziger Semitistische Studien*, herausgegeben von August Fischer und Heinrich Zimmern (Leipzig: J. C. Hinrichs, 1903 ff.).
73. H. Lenzen, *Die Entwicklung der Zikurrat von ihren Anfängen bis zur Zeit der III. Dynastie von Ur* (Leipzig: Otto Harrassowitz, 1941).
74. Günter Martiny, *Die Gegensätze im babylonischen und assyrischen Tempelbau*: Abhandlungen für die Kunde des Morgenlandes, XXI, 3 (Leipzig: F. A. Brockhaus, 1936).
75. Lubor Matouš, "Les contrats de vente d'immeubles provenant de Larsa," *Archiv orientální*, XVIII, 4 (1950), 11-67.
76. Bruno Meissner, *Babylonien und Assyrien* (Heidelberg: Carl Winter, 1920-1925) (citation in volume II).
77. Anton Moortgat, *Vorderasiatische Rollsiegel: Ein Beitrag zur Geschichte der Steinschneidekunst* (Berlin: Gebr. Mann, 1940).
78. David M. Myhrman, *Sumerian Administrative Documents Dated in the Reigns of the Kings of the Second Dynasty of Ur from the Temple Archives of Nippur Preserved in Philadelphia* (Philadelphia: Department of Archaeology, University of Pennsylvania, 1910).
79. Arnold Nöldeke, Arndt von Haller, Heinz Lenzen, and Ernst Heinrich, *Achter vorläufiger Bericht über die von der deutschen Forschungsgemeinschaft in Uruk-Warka unternommenen Ausgrabungen.* Cf. No. 44 (1936), No. 13 (1937).
80. A. Nöldeke, E. Heinrich and H. Lonzen, *Zehnter vorläufiger Bericht über die von der Deutschen Forschungsgemeinschaft in Uruk-Warka unternommenen Ausgrabungen.* Cf. No. 44 (1939), No. 2 (1939).
81. A. Leo Oppenheim, *Catalogue of the Cuneiform Tablets of the Wilberforce Eames Babylonian Collection in the New York Public Library: Tablets of the Time of the Third Dynasty of Ur*: American Oriental Series, XXXII (New Haven: American Oriental Society, 1948).
82. *Orientalia*, N.S.: Commentarii periodici Pontificii Instituti Biblici (Rome: Pontificium Institutum Biblicum, 1932 ff.).
83. José Ortega y Gasset, *Der Aufstand der Massen* (Stuttgart and Berlin: Deutsche Verlags-Anstalt, 1933).
84. A. Parrot, *Ziggurats et Tour de Babel* (1949).
85. Arno Poebel, *Historical and Grammatical Texts*: University of Pennsylvania. University Museum, Publications of the Babylonian section, V (Philadelphia: University Museum, 1914).
86. A. Pohl, "Eine neusumerische Achatperle," (82), XVI (1947), 464 ff.
87. — "Neue Ausgrabungen in Iraq," (82), XVIII, (1949), 124-30.

88. James B. Pritchard (editor), *Ancient Near Eastern Texts Relating to the Old Testament* (Princeton: Princeton University Press, 1950).
89. George Reisner, *Tempelurkunden aus Telloh*: Königliche Museen zu Berlin, Mitteilungen aus den orientalischen Sammlungen, XVI (Berlin: W. Spemann, 1901).
90. *Revue d'assyriologie et d'archéologie orientale* (Paris: Ernest Leroux, 1886 ff.).
91. Victor Scheil, *Une saison de fouilles à Sippar: Mémoires publiés par les membres de l'Institut Français d'archéologie orientale du Caire*, Teil I. (Cairo: Imprimerie de l'Institut, 1902).
92. Nikolaus Schneider, "Das Drehem- und Djohaarchiv," *Orientalia*: (a) 1. Heft, No. 8 (1924), (b) 2. Heft, No. 18 (1925), (c) 3. Heft, No. 22 (1926), (d) 5. Heft, No. 45-46 (1930).
93. — *Die Geschäftsurkunden aus Drehem und Djoha in den Staatlichen Museen (VAT) zu Berlin*: Orientalia, No. 47-49 (1930).
94. — *Die Götternamen von Ur III*: Analecta Orientalia, 19 (Rome: Pontificium Institutum Biblicum, 1939).
95. M. Schorr, *Urkunden des altbabylonischen Zivil- und Prozessrechts*: Vorderasiatische Bibliothek, 5 (Leipzig: J. C. Hinrichs, 1913).
96. J. J. Stamm, *Die akkadische Namengebung*: Mitteilungen der Vorderasiatischaegyptischen Gesellschaft, 44 (Leipzig: J. C. Hinrichs, 1939).
97. Francis Rue Steele, "The Date Formulae of Shu-ilishu of Isin," *Bulletin of the American Schools of Oriental Research*, 122 (April, 1951), 45-49.
98. François Thureau-Dangin, "La comptabilité agricole en Chaldée au troisième millénaire," (90), III (1895), 118-46.
99. — *Recueil de tablettes chaldéennes* (Paris: Ernest Leroux, 1903).
100. — *Die sumerischen und akkadischen Königsinschriften*: Vorderasiatische Bibliothek, 1 (Leipzig: J. C. Hinrichs, 1907).
101. — "Notes assyriologiques, V. La trouvaille de Dréhem," (90), VII (1910), 186-96.
102. — "La correspondance de Hammurabi avec Šamaš-hâṣir," (90), XXI (1924), 1-58.
103. Eckhard Unger, *Babylon die heilige Stadt nach der Beschreibung der Babylonier* (Berlin and Leipzig: Walter de Gruyter & Co., 1931).
104. Arthur Ungnad, *Babylonische Briefe aus der Zeit der Hammurabi-Dynastie*, Vorderasiatische Bibliothek, 6 (Leipzig: J. C. Hinrichs, 1914).
105. *The University of Chicago, Oriental Institute publications* (Chicago: University of Chicago Press, 1924 ff.).
106. Arnold Walther, *Das altbabylonische Gerichtswesen*, (72), VI, 4-6 (1917).
107. Ernst Weidner, "Bemerkungen zur Königsliste aus Chorsābād," (3), XV, (1945-1951).
108. — "Nippur," (3), XV (1945-1951), 140-41.
109. — "Nippur," (3), XVI, 1 (1952), 134.
110. *Yale Oriental series. Babylonian Texts* (New Haven: Yale University Press, 1915 ff.).
111. *Zeitschrift für Assyriologie und verwandte Gebiete* (ab Band 45: *und vorderasiatische Archäologie*) (Berlin: Walter de Gruyter & Co., Neue Folge: 1924 ff.).
112. H. Zimmern, "Ein Zyklus altsumerischer Lieder auf die Haupttempel Babyloniens," (111), XXXIX (1930), 245-76.

—